THE POWER OF
CONCENTRATION

T0144937

THE POWER OF CONCENTRATION

by Theron Q. Dumont

*The Classic to Harnessing
Your Mental Power*

From the Immortal Author of
The Kybalion

Abridged and Introduced
by Mitch Horowitz

THE CONDENSED CLASSICS LIBRARY™

MEDIA

Published by Gildan Media LLC
aka G&D Media.
www.GandDmedia.com

The Power of Concentration was originally published in 1916
G&D Media Condensed Classics edition published 2018
Abridgement and Introduction copyright © 2017 by Mitch
Horowitz

FIRST EDITION: 2018

Cover design by David Rheinhardt of Pyrographx

Interior design by Meghan Day Healey of Story Horse, LLC.

ISBN: 978-1-7225-0059-7

CONTENTS

The Voice of a Pioneer

If you're an avid reader of metaphysical books, as I am, you might find the voice in this valuable little volume, published in 1916, somewhat familiar.

It belongs to the remarkably energetic New Thought philosopher and publisher William Walker Atkinson, who wrote under several pseudonyms and produced nearly one hundred New Thought books in the three decades leading up to his death in 1932. The most popular of these works was *The Kybalion*, which Atkinson wrote under the name "Three Initiates" in 1908, eight years before this similarly enduring volume.

In *The Power of Concentration,* Atkinson used the name French name of Theron Q. Dumont, which was often his chosen byline to explore matters of psychology, willpower, suggestion, and self-hypnosis, all of which were closely associated with French thinkers in the early twentieth century. This was particularly the case with hypnosis, which was introduced in its earliest form in Paris in the late 1770s by occult healer Franz Anton Mesmer. Although the arrival of the France Revolution, and the ensuing years of social upheaval, interrupted the progress of hypnotic theory in France, the nation once more popularized the therapeutic uses of the craft in the late-nineteenth century through the so-called Nancy School of hypnotism, which promoted practices of suggestion and hypnotherapy. The Nancy movement produced the immensely popular French healer Emile Coué, who became famous in Europe and America in the 1910s and 20s for his self-help mantra, "Day by day, in every way, I am getting better and better."

This was the tradition to which Atkinson sought to attach himself with his persona Theron Q. Dumont. Under the name Dumont, he wrote several works on the power of personal magnetism, the uses of will and suggestion, and the self-shaping forces of the mind, of which *The Power of Concentration* is probably the most compelling, persuasive, and enduring.

As is often the case with Atkinson's works, the book is a feast of practicality and idealism. It is at once inspiring and hard-knuckled—there is no toleration for dreamy visualizations unmoored from outer action. Rather, *The Power of Concentration* shows how to harness your thoughts and habits to heighten your personal performance. Nearly every page contains injunctions to act, do, and strive.

The book's advice, reduced to its essentials in this condensation, remains potent and fresh more than a century after its publication. Atkinson's language often prefigures terms and concepts heard today in the fields of neuroplasticity and cognitive behavioral therapy. Yet his book contains an infectious dynamism and scale of purpose rarely found in either of those fields. The book captures both the epic hopes and the applicability of the early days of New Thought. Its techniques have never been eclipsed or surpassed.

—Mitch Horowitz

We all know that in order to accomplish a certain thing we must concentrate. It is of the utmost value to learn how to concentrate. To make a success of anything, you must be able to concentrate your entire thought upon the idea.

Do not become discouraged if you are unable to hold your thought on the subject very long at first. Very few can. It seems a peculiar fact that it is easier to concentrate on something that is *not* good for us than on something that is beneficial. This tendency is overcome when we learn to concentrate consciously.

Did you ever stop to think what an important part your thoughts play in your life? This book shows their far-reaching and all-abiding effects.

Man is a wonderful creature, but requires training and development to be useful. A great work can be accomplished by every man if he can be awakened to do his very best. But the greatest man would accomplish little if he lacked concentration and effort. Dwarfs can do the work of giants when they are transformed by the almost-magical power of great mental concentration. But giants will only do the work of dwarfs when they lack this power.

We accomplish more by concentration than by fitness; the man that is apparently best suited for a place does not always fill it best. It is the man who concentrates on every possibility that makes an art of both his work, and his life.

This course will stimulate and inspire you to achieve success; it will bring you into perfect harmony with the laws of success. It will give you a firmer hold on your duties and responsibilities.

The methods of thought-concentration given in this work, if put into practice, will open up interior avenues that will connect you with the everlasting laws of Being and their exhaustless foundation of unchangeable truth.

Concentration Finds the Way

Everyone has two natures. One wants to advance and the other wants to pull back. The one that we cultivate and concentrate on decides what we are at the end. Both natures are vying for control. The will alone decides the issue. A man by one supreme effort of the will may change his whole career, and almost accomplish miracles. You may be that man. You can be if you Will to be, for Will can find a way, or make one.

It is a matter of choice whether we allow our diviner self to control us, or whether we get controlled by the brute within. No man has to do anything he does not want to do. He is therefore the director of his life, if he wills to be. What we do is the result of our training. We are like putty, and can be completely controlled by our willpower.

Many people read good books, but say they do not get much out of them. They do not realize that all any

book or lesson can do is to awaken them to their possibilities. One of the most beneficial practices I know
of is looking for the good in everyone and everything,
for there is good in all things. We encourage a person
by seeing his good qualities, and we also help ourselves
by looking for them. We gain their good wishes, a most
valuable asset. We get back what we give out. The time
comes when most all of us need encouragement; need
buoying up. So, form the habit of encouraging others,
and you will find it a wonderful tonic for both others
and yourself, for you will get back encouraging and up-
lifting thoughts.

The first of each month, a person should sit down
and examine the progress he has made. If he has not
come up to expectations he should discover the reason,
and by extra exertion measure up to what is demanded.

I know that every man who is willing to pay the
price can be a success. The price is not in money, but in
effort. The first essential quality for success is the desire
to do—*to be something*. The next thing is to learn how
to do it; the next to carry it into execution. The man
best able to accomplish anything is the one with a broad
mind; a man may acquire knowledge that is foreign to
a particular case, but is, nevertheless, of some value in
all cases. So, the man who wants to be successful must
be liberal; he must acquire all the knowledge he can; he

must be well posted not only in one branch of his business but in every part of it. Such a man achieves success.

The secret of success is to try always to improve yourself no matter where you are or what your position. Learn all you can. Don't see how little you can do, but how much you can do. Such a man will always be in demand.

The man with grit and will may be poor today and wealthy in a few years; willpower is a better asset than money. Will will carry you over chasms of failure, if you but give it the chance.

Everyone *really wants* to do something, but few will put forward the effort to make the necessary sacrifice to secure it. There is only one way to accomplish anything, and that is to go ahead and do it. A man may accomplish almost anything today, if he just sets his heart on it and lets nothing interfere with his progress. Obstacles are quickly overcome by the man that sets out to accomplish his heart's desire. The "bigger" the man, the smaller the obstacle appears. The "smaller" the man the greater the obstacle appears. Always look at the advantage you gain by overcoming obstacles, and it will give you the needed courage for their conquest.

The Self-Mastery Power of Concentration

Man from a psychological standpoint of development is not what he should be. He does not possess the self-mastery, the self-directing power of concentration that is his right.

He has not trained himself to promote his self-mastery. Every balanced mind possesses faculties whose chief duties are to engineer, direct, and concentrate the operations of the mind, both in a mental and physical sense. Man must learn to control not only his mind but also his bodily movements.

When the self-regulating faculties are not developed the impulses, appetites, emotions, and passions have full swing, and the mind becomes impulsive, restless, emotional, and irregular. This makes mental concentration poor.

When the self-guiding faculties are weak, the person always lacks the power of mental concentration. Therefore, you cannot concentrate until you develop those very powers that *qualify* you to concentrate. If you cannot concentrate, one of the following is the cause:

1. Deficiency of the motor centers.
2. An impulsive and emotional mind.
3. An untrained mind.

The last fault can soon be removed by systematic practice. It is easiest to correct.

The impulsive and emotional state of mind can best be corrected by restraining anger, passion and excitement, hatred, strong impulses, intense emotions, fretfulness, etc. It is impossible to concentrate when you are in any of these excited states. You can help naturally decrease these by avoiding food and drinks as have nerve weakening or stimulating influences, or a tendency to stir up the passions, impulses, and emotions. It is also a good practice to watch and associate with people who are steady, calm, controlled, and conservative.

Many have the idea that when they get into a negative state they are concentrating, but this is not so. Their power of concentration becomes weaker, and they find it difficult to concentrate on anything. The mind that cannot center itself on a special subject or thought, is weak; as is the mind that cannot draw itself from a subject or thought. But the person who can center his mind on any problem, no matter what it is, and remove any unharmonious impressions, has strength of mind. Concentration, first, last, and all the time, means strength of mind.

A concentrated mind pays attention to thoughts, words, acts, and plans. The person who allows his mind to roam at will, will never accomplish a great deal in the world. He wastes his energies. You concentrate the moment you say, "I want to, I can, I will."

Concentration of the mind can only be developed by watching yourself closely. All kinds of development commence with close attention. You should regulate your every thought and feeling. When you commence to watch yourself, your own acts, and also the acts of other people, you use the faculties of autonomy, and, as you continue to do so, you improve your faculties, until in time you can engineer your every thought, wish, and plan. Only the trained mind can focalize. To hold a thought before it until all the faculties have had time to consider that thought is concentration.

The person who cannot direct his thoughts, wishes, plans, resolutions, and studies cannot possibly succeed to the fullest extent. The person who is impulsive one moment and calm the next has not the proper control over himself. He is not a master of his mind, nor of his thoughts, feelings, and wishes. Such a person cannot be a success. When he becomes irritated, he irritates others and spoils all chances of any concerned doing their best. But the person who can direct his energies and hold them at work in a concentrated manner controls his every work and act, and thereby gains power to control others. He can make his every move serve a useful end, and every thought a noble purpose.

He is consciously attentive and holds his mind to one thing at a time. He shuts out everything else. When you are talking to anyone give him your sole and undivided attention. Do not let your attention wander or be diverted. Give no heed to anything else, but make your will and intellect act in unison.

Start out in the morning and see how self-poised you can remain all day. At times, take an inventory of your actions during the day and see if you have kept your determination. If not, see that you do tomorrow. The more self-poised you are the better your concentration. Never be in too much of a hurry; and, remember, the more you improve your concentration, the greater are your possibilities. Concentration means success, because you are better able to govern yourself and centralize your mind; you become more in earnest in what you do, and this almost invariably improves your chances for success.

When you are talking to a person have your own plans in mind. Concentrate your strength upon the purpose you are talking about. Watch his every move, but keep your own plans before you. Unless you do, you will waste your energy and not accomplish as much as you should.

I want you to watch the next person you see who has the reputation of being a strong character, a man of force. Watch and see what a perfect control he has over his body. Then I want you to watch just an ordinary person. Notice how he moves his eyes, arms, fingers; notice the useless expenditure of energy. These movements lessen the person's power in vital and nerve directions. Center your mind on one purpose, one plan, one transaction.

There is nothing that uses up nerve force so quickly as excitement. This is why an irritable person is never magnetic; he is never admired or loved; he does not develop those finer qualities that a real gentleman possesses. Anger, sarcasm, and excitement weaken a person in this direction. The person that allows himself to get excited will become nervous in time, because he uses up his nerve forces and his vital energies. The person that cannot control himself and keep from becoming excited cannot concentrate.

But those whose actions are slower and directed by their intelligence develop concentration. Sometimes dogmatic, willful, excitable persons can concentrate, but it is spasmodic, erratic concentration instead of controlled and uniform concentration. Their energy works by spells; sometimes they have plenty, other times very little; it is easily excited; easily wasted. The best way to understand it is to compare it with the discharge of a gun. If the gun goes off when you want it to, it accomplishes the purpose, but if it goes off before you are ready, you not only waste ammunition, but are also likely to do some damage. That is just what most people do. They allow their energy to explode, thus not only wasting it, but also endangering others. They waste their power, their magnetism, and so injure their chance of success.

The brain is the storehouse of the energy. Most all persons have all the dynamic energy they need if they would concentrate it. They have the machine, but they must also have the engineer, or they will not go very far. The engineer is the self-regulating, directing power. The good engineer controls his every act. By what you do you either advance or degenerate. This is a good idea to keep always in mind. When you are uncertain whether you should do something, just think whether by doing it you will grow or deteriorate, and act accordingly.

I am a firm believer in "work when you work, play when you play." When you give yourself up to pleasure you can develop concentration by thinking of nothing else but pleasure; when your mind dwells on love, think of nothing but this and you will find you can develop a more intense love than you ever had before. When you concentrate your mind on the "you" or real self, and its wonderful possibilities, you develop concentration and a higher opinion of yourself. By doing this systematically, you develop power, because you cannot be systematic without concentrating on what you are doing. When you walk out into the country and inhale the fresh air, studying vegetation, trees, etc., you are concentrating. Whenever you fix your mind on a certain thought and hold your mind on it at successive intervals, you develop concentration.

If you hold your mind on some chosen object, you centralize your attention, just like the lens of the camera centralizes on a certain landscape. Therefore, always hold your mind on what you are doing, no matter what it is.

Practice inhaling long, deep breaths, not simply for the improvement of health, although that is no small matter, but also for the purpose of developing more power, more love, more life. All work assists in development.

If you want to get more out of life you must think more of love. Unless you have real affection for something, you have no sentiment, no sweetness, no magnetism. So arouse your love affections by your will, and enter into a fuller life.

The next time you feel yourself becoming irritable, use your will and be patient. This is a very good exercise in self-control. It will help you to keep patient if you will breathe slowly and deeply. If you find you are commencing to speak fast, just control yourself and speak slowly and clearly. Keep from either raising or lowering your voice, and concentrate on the fact that you are determined to keep your poise, and you will improve your power of concentration.

If you feel yourself getting irritable, nervous or weak, stand squarely on your feet with your chest up and inhale deeply, and you will see that your irritability will disappear and a silent calm will pass over you.

If you are in the habit of associating with nervous, irritable people, quit it until you grow strong in the power of concentration, because irritable, angry, fretful, dogmatic, and disagreeable people will weaken what powers of resistance you have.

When your eye is steady, your mind is steady. One of the best ways to study a person is to watch his physical movements, for, when we study his actions, we are studying his mind. Because actions are the expressions of the mind. As the mind is, so is the action. When you learn to control the body, you are gaining control over the mind.

How to Gain What You Want Through Concentration

The ignorant person may say, "How can you get anything by merely wanting it?" I say that through concentration you can get anything you want. Every desire can be gratified. But whether it is, will depend upon you concentrating to have that desire fulfilled. Merely wishing for something will not bring it. Wishing you had something shows a weakness, and not a belief that you will really get it. So never merely wish, as we are not living in a "fairy age." You use up just as much brain force in "vain imaginings" as you do when you think of something worthwhile.

Be careful of your desires, make a mental picture of what you want and set your will to this until it materializes. Never allow yourself to drift without helm or rudder. Know what you want to do, and strive with all your might to do it, and you will succeed.

Feel that you can accomplish anything you undertake. Many undertake to do things, but feel when they start they are going to fail, and usually they do. I will give an illustration. A man goes to a store for an article. The clerk says, "I am sorry, we do not have it." But the man that is determined to get that thing inquires if he doesn't know where he can get it. Again receiving an unsatisfactory answer the determined buyer consults the manager, and finally finds where the article can be bought.

That is the whole secret of concentrating on getting what you want. And, remember, your soul is a center of all-power, and you can accomplish what you will to. "I'll find a way or make one!" is the spirit that wins. I know a man who is now head of a large bank. He started there as a messenger boy. His father had a button made for him with a "P" on it and put it on his coat. He said, "Son, that 'P' is a reminder that some day you are to be the president of your bank. I want you to keep this thought in your mind. Every day do something that will put you nearer your goal." Each night after supper he would say, "Son, what did you do today?" In this way the thought was always kept in mind. He concentrated on becoming president of that bank, and he did. His father told him never to tell anyone what that "P" stood for. His associates made a good deal of fun of it. And they tried to find out what it stood for, but they never did until he was made president, and then he told the secret.

Don't waste your mental powers in wishes. Don't dissipate your energies by trying to satisfy every whim. Concentrate on doing something really worthwhile. The man that sticks to something is not the man that fails.

> *"Power to him who power exerts."*
> —Emerson

This great universe is interwoven with myriad forces. You make your own place, and whether it is important depends upon you. Through the Indestructible and Unconquerable Law you can, in time, accomplish all right things, and therefore do not be afraid to undertake whatever you really desire to accomplish and are willing to pay for in effort. *Anything that is right is possible.* That which is necessary will inevitably take place. If something is right, it is your duty to do it, though the whole world thinks it to be wrong.

"God and one are always a majority," or in plain words, that omnipotent interior law which is God, and the organism that represents you, is able to conquer the whole world if your cause is absolutely just. Don't say, "I wish I were great." You can do anything that is proper, and that you want to. Just say: You can. You will. You must. *Realize this* and the rest is easy.

The Silent Force That Produces Results

Through concentrated thought power you can make yourself whatever you please. By thought you can greatly increase your efficiency and strength. You are surrounded by all kinds of thoughts, some good, others bad, and you are sure to absorb some of the latter if you do not build up a positive mental attitude.

If you will study the needless moods of anxiety, worry, despondency, discouragement, and others that are the result of uncontrolled thoughts, you will realize how important the control of your thoughts are. Your thoughts make you what you are.

When I walk along the street and study the different people's faces I can tell how they spent their lives. It all shows in their faces, just like a mirror reflects their physical countenances. In looking in those faces I cannot help thinking how most of the people you see have wasted their lives.

Understanding the power of thought will awaken possibilities within you that you never dreamed of. Never forget that your thoughts are making your environment and your friends, and as your thoughts change these will also. The desire to do right carries with it a great power. I want you to thoroughly realize the importance of your thoughts, and how to make them valuable, to understand that your thoughts come to you over invisible wires and influence you.

In order to speak wisely you must secure at least a partial concentration of the faculties and forces upon the subject at hand. Speech interferes with the focusing powers of the mind, as it withdraws the attention to the external and therefore is hardly to be compared with that deep silence of the subconscious mind, where deep thoughts, and the silent forces of high potency, are evolved. It is necessary to be silent before you can speak wisely. The person who is really alert, well poised, and able to speak wisely under trying circumstances, is the person who has practiced in the silence. Most people do not know what the silence is and think it is easy to go into the silence, but this is not so. In the real silence, we become attached to that interior law and the forces become silent, because they are in a state of high potency. Hold the thought: In-silence-I-will-allow-my-higher-self-to-have-complete-control. I-will-be-true-to-my-higher-self. I-will-live-true-to-my-conception-of-what-is-right. I-realize-that-it-is-in-my-self-interest-to-live-up-to-my-best. I-demand-wisdom-so-that-I-may-act-wisely-for-myself-and-others.

In the next chapter, I tell you of the mysterious law that links all humanity together by the powers of co-operative thought, and chooses for us companionship and friends.

How Concentrated Thought
Links All Humanity

Success is the result of how you think. I will show you how to think to be successful.

The power to rule and attract success is within yourself. The barriers that shut these off from you are subject to your control. You have unlimited power to think, and this is the link that connects you with your omniscient source.

Success is the result of certain moods of mind or ways of thinking. These moods can be controlled by you, and produced at will.

Concentrated thought will accomplish seemingly impossible results and make you realize your fondest ambitions. At the same time that you break down barriers of limitation new ambitions will be awakened. If you will just realize that through deep concentration you become linked with thoughts of omnipotence, you will kill out entirely your belief in your limitations, and at the same time will drive away all fear and other negative and destructive thought forces, which constantly work against you.

It is just as easy to surround your life with what you want as it is with what you don't. It is a question to be decided by your will. There are no walls to prevent you from getting what you want, *providing you want what is right*. If you choose something that is not right, you are in opposition to the omnipotent plans of the universe, and deserve to fail. *But, if you base your desires on justice and good will, you avail yourself of the helpful powers of universal currents, and instead of having a handicap to work against, can depend upon ultimate success, though the outward appearances may not at first be bright.*

Never stop to think of temporary appearances, but maintain an unfaltering belief in your ultimate success. Make your plans carefully, and see that they are not contrary to the tides of universal justice. The main thing for you to remember is to keep at bay the destructive and opposing forces of fear, anger, and their satellites.

There is no power so great as the belief which comes from the knowledge that your thought is in harmony with the divine laws of thought, and the sincere conviction that your cause is right.

All just causes succeed in time, though temporarily they may fail. So if you should face the time when everything seems against you, quiet your fears, drive away all destructive thoughts, and uphold the dignity of your moral and spiritual life.

The following method may assist you in gaining better thought control. If you are unable to control your fears, just say to your faulty determination, "Do not falter or be afraid, for I am not really alone. I am surrounded by invisible forces that will assist me to remove the unfavorable appearances." Soon you will have more courage. The only difference between the fearless man and the fearful one is in his will, his hope. So if you lack success, believe in it, hope for it, claim it. You can use the same method to brace up your thoughts of desire, aspiration, imagination, expectation, ambition, understanding, trust, and assurance.

If you get anxious, angry, discouraged, undecided or worried, it is because you are not receiving the cooperation of the higher powers of your mind. By your Will you can so organize the powers of the mind that your moods change only as you want them to instead of as circumstances affect you. If you allow the mind to wander while you are doing small things, it will be likely to get into mischief and make it hard to concentrate on the important act when it comes.

The will does not act with clearness, decision and promptness *unless it is trained to do so.* Comparatively few people really know what they are doing every minute of the day. This is because they do not observe with sufficient orderliness and accuracy. It is not difficult to know what you are doing all the time, if you will just practice concentration, and with a reposeful deliberation train yourself to think clearly, promptly, and decisively.

If you allow yourself to worry or hurry in what you are doing, it will not be clearly photographed upon the sensitized plate of the subjective mind, and therefore you will not be really conscious of your actions. So practice accuracy and concentration of thought, and also absolute truthfulness, and you will soon be able to concentrate.

The Training of the Will to Do

The Will To Do is the greatest power in the world that is concerned with human accomplishment, and no one can predetermine its limits.

The Will To Do is a force that is strictly practical, yet it is difficult to explain just what it is. It can be compared to electricity because we know it only through its cause and effects. Every time you accomplish any definite act, consciously or unconsciously, you use the principle of the Will. You can Will to do anything, whether right or wrong, and therefore how you use your will makes a big difference in your life.

Every person possesses some "Will To Do." It is the inner energy that controls all conscious acts. *Genius is but a will to do little things with infinite pains. Little things done well open the door of opportunity for bigger things.*

Study yourself carefully. Find out your greatest weakness and then use your willpower to overcome it.

In this way eradicate your faults, one by one, until you have built up a strong character and personality.

Rules for Improvement. A desire arises. Now think whether this would be good for you. If it is not, use your Willpower to kill out the desire; but, on the other hand, if it is a righteous desire, summon all your Willpower to your aid, crush all obstacles that confront you, and secure possession of the coveted Good.

Slowness in Making Decisions. This is a weakness of Willpower. You know you should do something, but you delay doing it through lack of decision. It is easier not to do a certain thing , but conscience says to do it. The vast majority of people are failures because of the lack of deciding to do a thing when it should be done. Those that are successful have been quick to grasp opportunities by making a quick decision. This power of will can be used to bring culture, wealth, and health.

Some Special Pointers. For the next week try to make quicker decisions in your little daily affairs. Set the hour you wish to get up and arise exactly at the fixed time. Anything that you should accomplish, do on or ahead of time. You want, of course, to give due deliberation to weighty matters, but by making quick decisions on little things you will acquire the ability to make quick decisions in bigger things.

You Are as Good as Anyone. You have willpower, and if you use it, you will get your share of the luxuries of life. So use it to claim your own. Don't depend on anyone else to help you. We have to fight our own battles. All the world loves a fighter, while the coward is despised by all. Every person's problems are different, so I can only say "analyze your opportunities and conditions and study your natural abilities." Don't make an indefinite plan, but a definite one, and then don't give up until your object has been accomplished. Put these suggestions into practice with true earnestness, and you will soon note astonishing results, and your whole life will be completely changed. An excellent motto for one of pure motives is: *Through my willpower I dare do what I want to.* You will find this affirmation has a very strengthening effect.

The Spirit of Perseverance. The spirit of "stick-toitiveness" is the one that wins. Many go just so far and then give up, whereas, if they had persevered a little longer, they would have won out. Many have much initiative, but instead of concentrating it into one channel they diffuse it through several, thereby dissipating it to such an extent that its effect is lost.

Lack of Perseverance is nothing but the lack of the Will To Do. It takes the same energy to say, "I will continue," as to say, "I give up." Just the moment you say the latter you shut off your dynamo, and your determination is gone. Every time you allow your determination to be broken you weaken it. Don't forget this. Just the instant you notice your determination beginning to weaken, concentrate on it and by sheer Will Power make it continue on the "job."

Never try to make a decision when you are not in a calm state of mind. If in a "quick temper," you are likely to say things you regret. In anger, you follow impulse rather than reason. No one can expect to achieve success if he makes decisions when not in full control of his mental forces. Therefore make it a fixed rule to make decisions only when at your best.

Special Instructions to Develop the Will To Do. This is a form of mental energy, but requires the proper mental attitude to make it manifest. We hear of people having wonderful willpower, which really is wrong. It should be said that they *use* their willpower, while with many it is a latent force. I want you to realize that no one has a monopoly on willpower. What we speak of as willpower is but the gathering together of mental energy, the concentration of power at one point. So never think of someone as having a stronger will than you. Each person will be supplied with just that amount of willpower that he demands.

The Concentrated Mental Demand

The Mental Demand is the potent force in achievement. The attitude of the mind affects the expression of the face, determines action, changes our physical condition, and regulates our lives.

The mental demand must be directed by every power of the mind, and every possible element should be used to make the demand materialize. You can so intently desire a thing that you can exclude all distracting thoughts. When you practice this singleness of concentration until you attain the end sought, you have developed a Will capable of accomplishing whatever you wish.

The men looked upon as the world's successes have not always been men of great physical power, nor at the start did they seem very well adapted to the conditions around them. In the beginning, they were not considered men of superior genius, but they won their success by their resolution to achieve results by permitting no setback to dishearten them; no difficulties to daunt them. Nothing could turn them or influence them against their determination. They never lost sight of their goal. In all of us there is this silent force of wonderful power. If developed, it can overcome conditions that would seem insurmountable. It is constantly urging us on to greater achievement. The more we become acquainted with it the better strategists we become, the more courage we develop, and the greater the desire within us for self-expression along many lines.

No one will ever be a failure if he becomes conscious of this silent force within that controls his destiny. But without the consciousness of this inner force, you will not have a clear vision, and external conditions will not yield to the power of your mind. It is the mental resolve that makes achievement possible. Once this has been formed it should never be allowed to cease to press its claim until its object is attained.

Perseverance is the first element of success. In order to persevere you must be ceaseless in your application. It requires you to concentrate your thoughts upon your undertaking, and bring every energy to bear upon keeping them focused upon it until you have accomplished your aim. To quit short of this is to weaken all future efforts.

The Mental Demand seems an unreal power because it is intangible; but it is the mightiest power in the world. It is a power that is free for you to use. No one can use it for you. Every time you make a Mental Demand you strengthen the brain centers by drawing to you external forces.

Few realize the power of a Mental Demand. It is possible to make your demand so strong that you can impart what you have to say to another without speaking to him. Have you ever, after planning to discuss a certain matter with a friend, had the experience of having him broach the subject before you had a chance to speak of it? These things are neither coincidences nor accidents, but are the results of mental demand launched by strong concentration. The person that never wants anything gets little. To demand resolutely is the first step toward getting what you want.

Once the Mental Demand is made, however, never let it falter. If you do, the current that connects you with your desire is broken. Take all the necessary time to build a firm foundation, so that there need not be even an element of doubt to creep in. Just the moment you entertain "doubt" you lose some of the demand force, and force once lost is hard to regain. So whenever you make a mental demand hold steadfastly to it until your need is supplied.

And every man of AVERAGE ability, the ordinary man that you see about you, can be really successful, independent, free of worry, HIS OWN MASTER, if he can manage to do just two things: First, remain forever dissatisfied with what he IS doing and with what he HAS accomplished. Second, develop in his mind a belief that the word "impossible" was not intended for him. Build up in his mind the confidence that enables the mind to use its power.

Concentration
Gives Mental Poise

You will find that the man that concentrates is well poised, whereas the man that allows his mind to wander is easily upset. When in this state wisdom does not pass from the subconscious store-house into the consciousness. There must be mental quiet before the two forms of consciousness can work in harmony. When you are able to concentrate, you have peace of mind.

If you are in the habit of losing your poise, form the habit of reading literature that has a quieting power. Just the second you feel your poise slipping, say, "Peace," and then hold this thought in mind and you will never lose your self-control. Think of yourself as a child of the infinite, possessing infinite possibilities. Write on a piece of paper, "I have the power to do and to be whatever I wish to do and be." Keep this mentally before you, and you will find the thought will be of great help to you.

The Mistake of Concentrating on Your Business While Away. In order to be successful today, you must concentrate, but don't become a slave to concentration, and carry your business cares home. Just as sure as you do, you will be burning the life forces at both ends, and the fire will go out much sooner than intended.

Many men become so absorbed in their business that when they go to church they do not hear the preacher because their minds are on their business. If they go to the theater they do not enjoy it because their business is on their minds. When they go to bed they think about business instead of sleep. This is the wrong kind of concentration and is dangerous. It is involuntary. It is a big mistake to let a thought rule you, instead of ruling it. He who does not rule himself is not a success. If you cannot control your concentration, your health will suffer.

Never become so absorbed with anything that you cannot lay it aside and take up another. This is self-control. Concentration is paying attention to a chosen thought.

Self-Study Valuable. Everyone has some habits that can be overcome by concentration. We will say for instance, you are in the habit of complaining, or finding fault with yourself or others; or, imagining that you do not possess the ability of others; or feeling that you are not as good as someone else; or that you cannot rely on yourself; or harboring any similar thoughts. These should be cast aside, and instead thoughts of strength should be put in their place. Just remember that every time you think of yourself as being weak, in some way you are making yourself so. Our mental conditions make us what we are. Just watch yourself and see how much time you waste in worrying, fretting, and complaining. The more of it you do, the worse off you are.

Just the minute you are aware of thinking a negative thought immediately change to a positive one. If you start to think of failure, change to thinking of success. You have the germ of success within you. Care for it the same as the setting hen broods over the eggs, and you can make it a reality.

You can make those that you come in contact with feel as you do, because you radiate vibrations of the way you feel, and your vibrations are felt by others. When you concentrate on a certain thing you turn all the rays of your vibrations on this. Thought is the directing power of all Life's vibrations. If a person should enter a room with a lot of people and feel as if he were a person of no consequence, no one would know he was there unless they saw him; and even if they did, they would not remember seeing him, because they were not attracted towards him. But let him enter the room feeling that he was magnetic and concentrating on this thought, others would feel his vibration. So remember, the way you feel you can make others feel.

If you will study all of the great characters of history you will find that they were enthusiastic. First, they were enthusiastic themselves, and then they could arouse others' enthusiasm. It is latent in everyone. It is a wonderful force when once aroused. This is the keynote of success.

"Think, speak, and act just as you wish to be, And you will be that which you wish to be."

You are just what you think you are, and not what you may appear to be. You may fool others, but not yourself. You may control your life and actions just as you can control your hands. If you want to raise your hand, you must first think of raising it. If you want to control your life, you must first control your thinking. Easy to do, is it not? Yes it is, if you will but concentrate on what you think about.

How can we secure concentration? To this question, the first and last answer must be: by interest and strong motive. The stronger the motive, the greater the concentration.

Successful Lives Are the Concentrated Lives.
Train yourself so that you will be able to centralize
your thought, develop your brainpower, and increase
your mental energy, or you can be a slacker, a drifter,
a quitter, or a sleeper. It all depends on how you concentrate, or centralize your thoughts. Your thinking
then becomes a fixed power and you do not waste time
thinking about something that would not be good for
you. You pick out the thoughts that will be the means
of bringing you what you desire, and they become a material reality. Whatever we create in the thought world
will some day materialize. That is the law. Never forget
this.

**Why People Often Do Not Get What They Con-
centrate On.** Because they sit down in hopeless despair
and expect it to come to them. But if they will just reach
out for it with their biggest effort they will find it is
within their reach. No one limits us but ourselves.

Through our concentration we can attract what we
want, because we became en rapport with the Universal
forces, from which we can get what we want.

A man starts to think on a certain subject. He has
all kinds of thoughts come to him, but by concentration
he shuts out all these but the one he has chosen. Concentration is just a case of willing to do a certain thing,
and doing it.

If you want to accomplish anything, first put yourself in a concentrating, reposeful, receptive, acquiring frame of mind. In tackling unfamiliar work make haste slowly and deliberately, and then you will secure that interior activity, which is never possible when you are in a hurry or under a strain. When you "think hard," or try to hurry results too quickly, you generally shut off the interior flow of thoughts and ideas. You have often no doubt tried hard to think of something but could not, but just as soon as you stopped trying to think of it, it came to you.

Concentration Can Overcome Bad Habits

Habits make or break us to a far greater extent than we like to admit. Habit is both a powerful enemy and wonderful ally of concentration. You must learn to overcome habits that are injurious to concentration, and to cultivate those that increase it.

Most people are controlled by their habits, and are buffeted around by them like waves of the ocean tossing a piece of wood. They do things in a certain way because of the power of habit. They seldom ever think of concentrating on why they do them this or that way, or study to see if they could do them in a better way.

The first thing I want you to realize is that all habits are governed consciously or unconsciously by the will. Most of us are forming new habits all the time. Very often, if you repeat something several times in the same way, you will have formed the habit of doing it that way. But the oftener you repeat it the stronger that habit grows, and the more deeply it becomes embedded in your nature. After a habit has been in force for a long time, it becomes almost a part of you, and is therefore hard to overcome. But you can still break any habit by strong concentration on its opposite.

You will find the following maxims worth remembering.

First Maxim: "We must make our nervous system our ally instead of our enemy."

Second Maxim: "In the acquisition of a new habit as in the leaving off of an old one, we must take care to launch ourselves with as strong and decided an initiative as possible."

Surround yourself with every aid you can. Don't play with fire by forming bad habits. Make a new beginning today. Study why you have been doing certain things. If they are not for your good, shun them henceforth. Don't give in to a single temptation, for every time you do, you strengthen the chain of bad habits. Every time you keep a resolution you break the chain that enslaves you.

Third Maxim: "Never allow an exception to occur till the new habit is securely rooted in your life."

Fourth Maxim: "Seize the very first possible opportunity to act on every resolution you make, and on every emotional prompting you may experience in the direction of the habits you aspire to gain."

Keep every resolution you make, for you not only profit by the resolution, but it furnishes you with an exercise that causes the brain cells and physiological correlatives to form the habit of adjusting themselves to carry out resolutions. A tendency to act becomes effectively engrained in us in proportion to the uninterrupted frequency with which the actions actually occur, and the brain "grows" to their use.

Fifth Maxim: "Keep the faculty of effort alive in you by a little gratuitous exercise every day."

The more we exercise the will, the better we can control our habits. Every few days, do something for no other reason than its difficulty, so that when the hour of dire need draws near, it may find you not unnerved or untrained to stand the test. Asceticism of this sort is like the insurance that a man pays on his house and goods. So with the man who has daily insured himself to habits of concentrated attention, energetic volition, and self-denial in unnecessary things.

Habits have often been called a labor-saving invention, because when they are formed they require less of both mental and material strength. The more deeply the habit becomes ingrained, the more automatic it becomes. Therefore habit is an economizing tendency of our nature, for if it were not for habit we should have to be more watchful. We walk across a crowded street; the habit of stopping and looking prevents us from being hurt. Habits mean less risk, less fatigue, and greater accuracy.

In order to overcome undesirable habits, two things are necessary. You must have trained your will to do what you want it to do, and the stronger the will the easier it will be to break a habit. Then you must make a resolution to do just the opposite of what the habit is. I will bring this chapter to a close by giving Doctor Oppenheim's instructions for overcoming a habit:

"If you want to abolish a habit, and its accumulated circumstances as well, you must grapple with the matter as earnestly as you would with a physical enemy. You must go into the encounter with all tenacity of determination, with all fierceness of resolve—and yea, even with a passion for success that may be called vindictive.

No human enemy can be as insidious, so persevering, as unrelenting as an unfavorable habit. It never sleeps, it needs no rest.

"It is like a parasite that grows with the growth of the supporting body, and, like a parasite, it can best be killed by violent separation and crushing."

It is not in the easy, contented moments of our life that we make our greatest progress, for then it requires no special effort to keep in tune. But it is when we are in the midst of trials and misfortunes, when we think we are sinking, being overwhelmed, then it is important for us to realize that we are linked to a great Power, and if we live as we should, there is nothing that can occur in life that could permanently injure us, nothing can happen that should disturb us. Always remember you have within you unlimited power, ready to manifest itself in the form which fills our need at the moment.

Business Results Through Concentration

Business success depends on well-concentrated efforts. You must use every mental force you can master. The more these are used, the more they increase. Therefore the more you accomplish today the more force you will have at your disposal to solve your problems tomorrow. Then when you have resolved what you want to do, you will be drawn towards it. There is a law that opens the way to the fulfillment of your desires. Of course, back of your desire you must put forward the necessary effort to carry out your purpose; you must use your power to put your desires into force. Once they are created, and you keep up your determination to have them fulfilled, you both consciously and unconsciously work toward their materialization. Set your heart on your purpose, concentrate your thought upon it, direct your efforts with all your intelligence, and in due time you will realize your ambition.

Feel yourself a success, believe you are a success, and thus put yourself in the attitude that demands recognition and the thought current draws to you what you need to make you a success. Don't be afraid of big undertakings. Go at them with grit, and pursue methods that you think will accomplish your purpose. You may not at first meet with entire success, but aim so high that if you fall a little short you will still have accomplished much.

What others have done you can do. You may even do what others have been unable to do. Always keep a strong desire to succeed in your mind. Be in love with your aim and work, and make it, as far as possible, square with the rule of the greatest good to the greatest number, and your life cannot be a failure.

The successful business attitude must be cultivated to make the most out of your life: the attitude of expecting great things from both yourself and others. This alone will often cause men to make good; to measure up to the best that is in them.

It is not the spasmodic spurts that count on a long journey, but the steady efforts. Spurts fatigue, and make it hard for you to continue.

When once you reach a conclusion abide by it. Let there be no doubt, or wavering. If you are uncertain about every decision you make, you will be subject to harassing doubts and fears, which will render your judgment of little value. The man that decides according to what he thinks right, and who learns from every mistake, acquires a well-balanced mind that gets the best results. He gains the confidence of others. He is known as the man who knows what he wants, and not as one that is as changeable as the weather. Reliable firms want to do business with men of known qualities, with men of firmness, judgment, and reliability.

So, if you wish to start in business for yourself, your greatest asset, with the single exception of a sound physique, is that of a good reputation.

A successful business is not hard to build if we can concentrate all our mental forces upon it. We hear people say that business is trying on the nerves, but it is the unsettling elements of fret, worry, and suspense that are nerve exhausting, and not the business. Executing one's plans may cause fatigue, but enjoyment comes with rest. If there has not been any unnatural strain, the recuperative powers replace what energy has been lost.

By attending to each day's work properly, you develop the capacity to do a greater work tomorrow. It is this gradual development that makes possible the carrying out of big plans.

Even brilliant men's conceptions of the possibilities of their mental forces are so limited and below their real worth that they are far more likely to belittle their possibilities than they are to exaggerate them. You don't want to think that an aim is impossible because it has never been realized in the past. Everyday someone is doing something that was never done before.

The natural leader always draws to himself, by the law of mental attraction, all the ideas in his chosen subject that have ever been conceived by others. This is of the greatest importance and help. If you are properly trained you benefit much by others' thoughts, and, providing you generate from within yourself something of value, they will benefit from yours. "We are heirs of all the ages," but we must know how to use our inheritance.

The confident, pushing, hopeful, determined man influences all with whom he associates, and inspires the same qualities in them. There is no reason why your work or business should burn you out. When it does, something is wrong. You are attracting forces and influence that you should not, because you are not in harmony with what you are doing. There is nothing so tiring as trying to do work for which we are unfitted both by temperament and training.

Each one should be engaged in a business that he loves; he should be furthering movements with which he is in sympathy. Only then will he do his best, and take intense pleasure in his business. In this way, while constantly growing and developing his powers, he is at the same time rendering through his work genuine and devoted service to humanity.

Concentrate On Your Courage

Courage is the backbone of man. The man with courage has persistence. He states what he believes, and puts it into execution.

Lack of courage creates financial, as well as mental and moral difficulties. When a new problem comes, instead of looking upon it as something to be achieved, the man or woman without courage looks for reasons why it cannot be done, and failure is naturally the almost inevitable result. This is a subject well worth your study. Look upon everything within your power as a possibility, and you will accomplish a great deal more, because by considering a thing as impossible you immediately draw to yourself all the elements that contribute to failure. Lack of courage destroys your confidence in yourself.

The man without courage unconsciously draws to himself all that is contemptible, weakening, demoralizing, and destructive. We must first have the courage to *strongly desire something*. A desire to be fulfilled must be backed by the strength of all our mental forces. Such a desire has enough commanding force to change all unfavorable conditions.

What is courage? It is the *Will To Do*. It takes no more energy to be courageous than to be cowardly. It is a matter of the right training, in the right way. Courage concentrates the mental forces on the task at hand. It then directs them thoughtfully, steadily, deliberately, while attracting all the forces of success toward the desired end.

As we are creatures of habits, we should avoid people who lack courage. They are easy to discover because of their habits of fear in attacking new problems. The man with courage is never afraid.

Start out today with the idea that there is no reason why you should not be courageous. If any fear-thoughts come to you, cast them off as you would the deadly viper. Form the habit of never thinking of anything unfavorable to yourself or anyone else. In dealing with difficulties, new or old, hold ever the thought: "I am courageous." Whenever a doubt crosses the threshold of your mind, banish it. Remember, you as master of your mind control its every thought, and here is a good one to often affirm: "I have courage because I desire it;

because I need it; because I use it; and because I refuse to become such a weakling as cowardice produces."

There is no justification for the loss of courage. The evils by which you will almost certainly be overwhelmed without it are far greater than those which courage will help you to meet and overcome. Right, then, must be the moralist who says that the only thing to fear is fear.

Never let another's opinion affect you; he cannot tell what you are able to do; he does not know what you can do with your forces. The truth is, you do not know yourself until you put yourself to the test. Therefore, how can someone else know? Never let anyone else put a valuation on you.

Almost all wonderful achievements have been accomplished after it had been "thoroughly" demonstrated that they were impossibilities. Once we understand the law, all things are possible. If they were impossibilities, we could not conceive them.

Just the moment you allow someone to influence you against what you think is right, you lose that confidence that inspires courage and carries with it all the forces that courage creates. Just the moment you begin to swerve in your plan you begin to carry out another's thought, and not your own. You become the directed and not the director. You forsake the courage and resolution of your own mind, and you therefore lack the very forces that you need to sustain and carry out your work. Instead of being self-reliant you become timid, and this invites failure. When you permit yourself to be influenced from your plan by another, you are unable to judge as you should, because you have allowed another's influence to deprive you of your courage and determination without absorbing any of his in return, so you are in much the same predicament as you would be in if you turned over all your worldly possessions to another without getting value received.

Concentrate on just the opposite of fear, want, poverty, sickness, etc. Never doubt your own ability. You have plenty, *if you will just use it.* A great many men are failures because they doubt their own capacity. Instead of building up strong mental forces, which would be of the greatest use to them, their fear thoughts tear them down. Fear paralyzes energy. It keeps us from attracting the forces that make success. Fear is the worst enemy we have.

Few people really know that they can accomplish much. They desire the full extent of their powers, but alas, it is only occasionally that you find a man who is aware of the great possibilities within him. When you believe with all your mind and heart and soul that you can do something, you thereby develop the courage to steadily and confidently live up to that belief. You have now gone a long way towards accomplishing it. Strong courage eliminates the injurious and opposing forces by summoning their masters, the yet-stronger forces that will serve you.

Courage is yours for the asking. All you have to do is to believe in it, claim it, and use it. One man of courage can fire with his spirit a whole army of men, whether military or industrial, because courage, like cowardice, is contagious.

Concentrate on Wealth

It was never intended that man should be poor. When wealth is obtained under the proper conditions, it broadens the life. Everything has its value. Everything has a good use and a bad use. The forces of mind, like wealth, can be directed either for good or evil. A little rest will re-create forces. Too much rest degenerates into laziness, and brainless, dreamy longings.

So, the first step toward acquiring wealth is to surround yourself with helpful influences; to claim for yourself an environment of culture, place yourself in it, and be molded by its influences.

Wealth is usually the fruit of achievement. It is not, however, altogether the result of being industrious. Thousands of persons work hard who never grow wealthy. Others with much less effort acquire wealth. Seeing possibilities is another step toward acquiring wealth. A man may be as industrious as he can possibly be, but if he does not use his mental forces he will be a laborer, to be directed by the man who uses to good advantage his mental forces.

No one can become wealthy in an ordinary lifetime by mere savings from earnings. Many scrimp and economize all their lives; but by so doing waste all their vitality and energy. For example, I know a man who used to walk to work. It took him an hour to go and an hour to return. He could have taken a car and gone in twenty minutes. He saved ten cents a day, but wasted an hour and a half. It was not a very profitable investment, unless the time spent in physical exercise yielded him large returns in the way of health.

The same amount of time spent in concentrated effort to overcome his unfavorable business environment might have firmly planted his feet in the path of prosperity.

One of the big mistakes made by many people is that they associate with those who fail to call out or develop the best that is in them. When the social side of life is developed too exclusively, and recreation or entertainment becomes the leading motive of a person's life, he acquires habits of extravagance instead of economy; habits of wasting his resources, physical, mental, moral, and spiritual, instead of conserving them.

The other day I attended a lecture on Prosperity. I knew the lecturer had been practically broke for ten years. I wanted to hear what he had to say. He spoke very well. He no doubt benefited some of his hearers, but he had not profited by his own teachings. I introduced myself and asked him if he believed in his maxims. He said he did. I asked him if they had made him prosperous. He said not exactly. I asked him why. He answered that he thought he was fated not to experience prosperity.

In half an hour, I showed that man why poverty had always been his companion. He had dressed poorly. He held his lectures in poor surroundings. By his actions and beliefs he attracted poverty. He did not realize that his thoughts and his surroundings exercised an unfavorable influence. I said: "Thoughts are moving forces; great powers. Thoughts of wealth attract wealth. Therefore, if you desire wealth you must attract the forces that will help you to secure it. Your thoughts attract a similar kind of thoughts. If you hold thoughts of poverty you attract poverty. If you make up your mind you are going to be wealthy, you will instill this thought into all your mental forces, and you will at the same time use every external condition to help you."

Business success depends on foresight, good judgment, grit, firm resolution, and settled purpose. But never forget that thought is as real a force as electricity. Let your thoughts be such that you will send out as good as you receive; if you do not, you are not enriching others, and therefore deserve not to be enriched.

Again I repeat that the first as well as the last step in acquiring wealth is to surround yourself with good influences—good thought, good health, good home and business environment, and successful business associates. Cultivate, by every legitimate means, the acquaintance of men of big caliber. Bring your thought vibrations in regard to business into harmony with theirs. This will make your society not only agreeable, but sought after, and, when you have formed intimate friendships with clean, reputable men of wealth, entrust to them, for investment, your surplus earnings, however small, until you have developed the initiative and business acumen to successfully manage your own investments. By this time you will, through such associations, have found your place in life which, if you have rightly concentrated upon and used your opportunities, will not be among men of small parts.

There is somewhere in every brain the energy that will get you out of that rut and put you far up on the mountain of success, if you can only use the energy. And hope, self-confidence, and the determination to do something supply the spark that makes the energy work.

You Can Concentrate, But Will You?

All have the ability to concentrate, but will you? You can, but whether you will or not depends on you. It is one thing to be able to do something, another to do it. There is far more ability not used than is used. Why do not more men of ability make something of themselves? There are comparatively few successful men, but many ambitious ones. Why do not more get along? Cases may differ, but the fault is usually their own. They have had chances, perhaps better ones than some others that have made good.

What would you like to do that you are not doing? If you think you should be "getting on" better, why don't you? Study yourself carefully. Learn your shortcomings. Sometimes only a mere trifle keeps one from branching out and becoming a success. Discover why you have not been making good—the cause of your failure. Have you been expecting someone to lead you, or to make a way for you? If you have, concentrate on a new line of thought.

There are two things absolutely necessary for success—energy and the will to succeed. Nothing can take the place of either of these.

When we see those with handicaps amounting to something great in the world, the able-bodied man should feel ashamed of himself if he does not make good. There is nothing that can resist the force of perseverance. The way ahead for all of us is not clear sailing, but all hard passages can be bridged.

Many men will not begin an undertaking unless they feel sure they will succeed in it. What a mistake! This would be right, if we were sure of what we could and could not do. But who knows? *There may be an obstruction there now that might not be there next week. There may not be an obstruction there now that will be there next week.* The trouble with most people is that just as soon as they see their way blocked they lose courage. They forget that usually there is a way around the difficulty. It's up to you to find it. If you tackle something with little effort, when the conditions call for a big effort, you will, of course, not win. Tackle everything with a feeling that you will use all the power within you to make it a success. This is the kind of concentrated effort that succeeds.

Most people are beaten before they start. They think they are going to encounter obstacles, and they look for them instead of for means to overcome them. The result is that they increase their obstacles instead of diminishing them. Have you ever undertaken something that you thought would be hard, but afterwards found it easy? That is the way a great many times. Things that look difficult in advance turn out to be easy of conquest when once encountered. So start out on your journey with the idea that the road is going to be clear for you, and that if it is not you will clear the way.

The one great keynote of success is to do whatever you have decided on. Don't be turned from your path, but resolve that you are going to accomplish what you set out to do. Don't be frightened at a few rebuffs, for they cannot stop the man that is determined—the man that knows in his heart that success is only bought by tremendous resolution, by concentrated and whole-hearted effort.

It is not so much skill that wins victories, as it is activity and great determination. There is no such thing as failure for the man who does his best. No matter what you may be working at, don't let this make you lose courage. *The tides are continually changing, and to-*

morrow or some other day they will turn to your advantage if you are a willing and ambitious worker. There is nothing that develops you and increases your courage like work. If it were not for work how monotonous life would become!

So I say to the man who wants to advance: "Don't look upon your present position as your permanent one. Keep your eyes open, and add those qualities to your makeup that will assist you when your opportunity comes. Be ever alert and on the watch for opportunities. Remember, we attract what we set our minds on. If we look for opportunities, we find them."

The Art of Concentration with Practical Exercises

Select some thought, and see how long you can hold your mind on it. It is well to have a clock at first and keep track of the time. If you decide to think about health, you can get a great deal of good from your thinking besides developing concentration. Think of health as being the greatest blessing in the world. Don't let any other thought drift in. The moment one starts to obtrude, make it get out.

Make it a daily habit of concentrating on this thought for, say, ten minutes. Practice until you can hold it to the exclusion of everything else. You will find it of the greatest value to centralize your thoughts on health. Regardless of your present condition, see yourself as you would like to be, and be blind to everything else. You will find it hard at first to forget your ailments, if you have any, but after a short while you can shut out these negative thoughts and see yourself as you want to be. Each time you concentrate, you form a more perfect image of health, and, as you come into its realization, you become healthy, strong, and wholesome.

I want to impress upon your mind that the habit of forming mental images is of the greatest value. It has always been used by successful men of all ages, but few realize its full importance.

Do you know that you are continually acting according to the images you form? If you allow yourself to mold negative images, you unconsciously build a negative disposition. You will think of poverty, weakness, disease, fear, etc., just as surely as you think of these will your objective life express itself in a like way. Just what we think, we will manifest in the external world.

In deep concentration you become linked with the great creative spirit of the universe, and the creative energy then flows through you, vitalizing your creations into form. In deep concentration your mind becomes attuned with the infinite and registers the cosmic intelligence and receives its messages. You become so full of the cosmic energy that you are flooded with divine power. This is a most desired state. It is then we realize the advantages of being connected with the supra-consciousness. The supra-consciousness registers the higher cosmic vibrations. It is often referred to as the wireless station, the message recorded coming from the universal mind.

Watch yourself during the day and see that your muscles do not become tense or strained. See how easy and relaxed you can keep yourself. See how poised you can be at all times. Cultivate a self-poised manner, instead of a nervous, strained appearance. This mental feeling will improve your carriage and demeanor. Stop all useless gestures and movements of the body. These mean that you have not proper control over your body. After you have acquired this control, notice how "ill-at-ease" people are that have not gained this control.

Get rid of any habit you have of twitching or jerking any part of your body. You will find that you make many involuntary movements. You can quickly stop any of these by merely centering your attention on the thought: "I will not."

No matter what you may be doing, imagine that it is your chief object in life. Imagine you are not interested in anything else in the world but what you are doing. Do not let your attention get away from the work you are at. Your attention will no doubt be rebellious, but control it, and do not let it control you.

When once you conquer the rebellious attention, you have achieved a greater victory than you can realize at the time.

By concentration you can control your temper. If you are one of those that flare up at the slightest "provocation" and never try to control yourself, just think this over a minute. Does it do you any good? Do you gain anything by it? Doesn't it put you out of poise for some time? Don't you know that this grows on you, and will eventually make you despised by all that have any dealings with you?

Many of you that read this may think you are not guilty of either of these faults, but if you will carefully watch yourself, you will probably find that you are, and, if so, you will be greatly helped by repeating this affirmation each morning:

"I am going to try today not to make a useless gesture or to worry over trifles, or become nervous or irritable. I intend to be calm, and, no difference what may be the circumstances, I will control myself. Henceforth, I resolve to be free from all signs that show lack of self-control."

Now, a word on needless talking. It seems natural to want to tell others what you know; but, by learning to control these desires, you can wonderfully strengthen your powers of concentration. Remember, you have all you can do to attend to your own business. Do not waste your time in thinking of others, or in gossiping about them.

If, from your own observation, you learn something about another person that is detrimental, keep it to yourself. Your opinion may afterwards turn out to be wrong anyway; but whether right or wrong, you have strengthened your will by controlling your desire to communicate your views.

If you hear good news, resist the desire to tell it to the first person you meet and you will be benefited thereby. It will require the concentration of all your powers of resistance to prohibit the desire to tell. After you feel that you have complete control over your desires, you can then tell your news. But you must be able to suppress the desire to communicate the news until you are fully ready to tell it. Persons that do not possess this power of control over desires are apt to tell things that they should not, thereby often involving both themselves and others in needless trouble.

If you are in the habit of getting excited when you hear unpleasant news, just control yourself and receive it without any exclamation of surprise. Say to yourself, "Nothing is going to cause me to lose my self-control." You will find from experience that this self-control will be worth much to you in business. You will be looked upon as a cool-headed businessman, and this in time becomes a valuable asset. Of course, circumstances alter cases. At times it is necessary to become enthused. But be ever on the lookout for opportunities for the practice of self-control. "He that ruleth his spirit is greater than he that ruleth a city."

Concentrate So You Will Not Forget

We remember only that which makes a deep impression; hence we must first deepen our impressions by associating in our minds certain ideas that are related to them.

Let's say a wife gives her husband a letter to mail. He does not think about it, but automatically puts it in his pocket and forgets all about it. When the letter was given to him had he said to himself, "I will mail this letter. The box is at the next corner and when I pass it I must drop this letter," it would have enabled him to recall the letter the instant he reached the mailbox.

The same rule holds good in regard to more important things. For example, if you are instructed to drop in and see Mr. Smith while out to lunch today, you will not forget it, if, at the moment the instruction is given, you say to yourself something similar to this: "When I get to the corner of Blank Street, on my way to lunch, I shall turn to the right and call on Mr. Smith." In this way the impression is made, the connection established, and the sight of the associated object recalls the errand.

The important thing to do is to deepen the impression at the very moment it enters your mind. This is made possible not only by concentrating the mind upon the idea itself, but by surrounding it with all possible association of ideas, so that each one will reinforce the others.

The mind is governed by laws of association, such as the law that ideas that enter the mind at the same time emerge at the same time, one assisting in recalling the others. You can train yourself to remember in this way by the concentration of the attention on your purpose, in accordance with the laws of association.

How Concentration Can Fulfill Your Desire

It is a spiritual law that the desire to do necessarily implies the ability to do."

All natural desires can be realized. It would be wrong for the Infinite to create wants that could not be supplied. Man's very soul is in his power to think, and it, therefore, is the essence of all created things. Every instinct of man leads to thought, and in every thought there is great possibility because true thought development, when allied to those mysterious powers which perhaps transcend it, has been the cause of all the world's true progress.

Silent, concentrated thought is more potent than spoken words, for speech distracts from the focusing power of the mind by drawing more and more attention to the without.

Man must learn more and more to depend on himself; to seek more for the Infinite within. It is from this source alone that he gains the power to solve his practical difficulties. No one should give up when there is always the resources of Infinity. The cause of failure is that men search in the wrong direction for success, because they are not conscious of their real powers, which when used are capable of guiding them.

The Infinite within is foreign to those who go through life without developing their spiritual powers. But the Infinite helps only he who helps himself. There is no such thing as a Special "Providence." Man will not receive help from the Infinite except to the extent that he believes and hopes and prays for help from this great source.

Remember that the first step in concentration is to form a Mental Image of what you wish to accomplish. This image becomes a thought-seed that attracts thoughts of a similar nature. Around this thought, when it is once planted in the imagination or creative region of the mind, you group or build associated thoughts, which continue to grow as long as your desire is keen enough to compel close concentration.

Form the habit of thinking of something you wish to accomplish for five minutes each day. Shut every other thought out of consciousness. Be confident that you will succeed; make up your mind that all obstacles will be overcome, and that you can rise above any environment.

A great aid in the development of concentration is to write out your thoughts on that which lies nearest your heart and to continue, little by little, to add to it until you have as nearly as possible exhausted the subject. You will find that each day as you focus your forces on this thought at the center of the stream of consciousness, new plans, ideas, and methods will flash into your mind.

We can attract those things that will help us. Very often we seem to receive help in a miraculous way. It may be slow in coming, but once the silent unseen forces are put into operation, they will bring results so long as we do our part. By forming a strong mental image of your desire, you plant the thought-seed that begins working in your interest and, in time, that desire, if in harmony with your higher nature, will materialize.

It may seem that it would be unnecessary to caution you to concentrate only upon achievement that will be good for you, and work no harm to another, but there are many who forget others and their rights, in their anxiety to achieve success. All good things are possible for you to have, but only as you bring your forces into harmony with that law that requires that we mete out justice to fellow travelers as we journey along life's road. So first think over the thing wanted and if it would be good for you to have. Say: "I want to do this; I am going to work to secure it. The way will be open for me."

If you fully grasp mentally the thought of success and hold it in mind each day, you gradually make a pattern or mold, which in time will materialize. But by all means keep free from doubt and fear, the destructive forces. Never allow these to become associated with your thoughts.

At last you will create the desired conditions, and receive help in many unlooked-for ways that will lift you out of the undesired environment. Life will then seem very different to you, for you will have found happiness through awakening within yourself the power to become the master of circumstances, instead of their slave.

Remember the mystical words of Jesus, the Master: "Whatsoever thing ye desire when ye pray, pray as if ye had already received and ye shall have."

Ideals Developed by Concentration

We often hear people spoken of as idealists. The fact is we are all idealists to a certain extent, and upon the ideals we picture depend our ultimate success. You must have the mental image if you are to produce the material thing. Everything is first created in the mind. When you control your thoughts, you become a creator. You receive divine ideas and shape them to your individual needs. All things of this world are to you just what you think they are. Your happiness and success depend upon your ideals.

Concentrate Upon Your Ideals and They Will Become Material Actualities. Through concentration we work out our ideals in physical life. Your future depends upon the ideals you are forming now. Your past ideals are determining your present. Therefore, if you want a bright future, you must begin to prepare for it today.

We say that a man is as changeable as the weather. What is meant is his ideals change. Every time you change your ideal you think differently. You become like a rudderless boat on an ocean. Therefore realize the importance of holding to your ideal until it becomes a reality.

You get up in the morning determined that nothing will make you lose your temper. This is your ideal of a person of real strength and poise. Something takes place that upsets you completely, and you lose your temper. For the time being you forget your ideal. If you had just thought a second of what a well-poised person implies you would not have become angry. *You lose your poise when you forget your ideal.* Each time we allow our ideals to be shattered we also weaken our willpower. Holding to your ideals develops willpower. Never forget this.

Why do so many fail? Because they don't hold to their ideal until it becomes a mental habit. When they concentrate on it to the exclusion of all other things, it becomes a reality. "I am that which I think myself to be."

You must give some hours to concentrated, consistent, persistent thought. You must study yourself and your weaknesses.

No man gets over a fence by wishing himself on the other side. He must climb.

No man gets out of the rut of dull, tiresome, monotonous life by merely wishing himself out of the rut. He must climb.

If you are standing still, or going backward, there is something wrong. You are the person to find out what is wrong.

Don't think that you are neglected, or not understood, or not appreciated.

Such thoughts are the thoughts of failure.

You know that the only thing in the world that you have got to count upon is yourself.

Concentration Reviewed

In this closing chapter, I want to impress you to concentrate on what you do, instead of performing most of your work unconsciously or automatically, until you have formed habits that give you the mastery of your work, and your life powers and forces.

Very often the hardest part of work is thinking about it. When you get right into it, it does not seem so disagreeable. This is the experience of many when they first commence to learn how to concentrate. So never think it a difficult task, but undertake it with the "I Will Spirit," and you will find that its acquirement will be as easy as its application will be useful.

Read the life of any great man, and you will generally find that the dominant quality that made him successful was the ability to concentrate. Study those who have been failures, and you will often find that lack of concentration was the cause.

Never say, "I can't concentrate today." You can do it just the minute you say, "I will." You *can* keep your thoughts from straying, just the same as you can control your arms. Once you realize this fact, you can train the will to concentrate on anything you wish. If it wanders, it is your fault. You are not using your will. But don't blame it on your will, and say it is weak. The will is the same whether you act as if it were weak or as if it were strong. When you act as if your will is strong you say, "I can." When you act as if it were weak you say, "I can't." It requires the same amount of effort.

Some men get in the habit of thinking, "I can't," and they fail. Others think, "I can," and succeed. So remember, it is for you to decide whether you will join the army of "I can't" or "I can."

The big mistake with so many is that they don't realize that when they say, "I can't," they really say, "I won't try." You cannot tell what you can do until you try. "Can't" means you will not try.

Before going to bed tonight, repeat: "I am going to choose my own thoughts, and to hold them as long as I choose. I am going to shut out all thoughts that weaken or interfere, that make me timid. My Will is as strong as anyone else's." While going to work the next morning, repeat this Keep this up for a month, and you will find you will have a better opinion of yourself. These are the factors that make you a success. Hold fast to them always.

Concentration is nothing but willing to do a certain thing. All foreign thoughts can be kept out by willing that they stay out. You cannot realize your possibilities until you commence to direct your mind.

You have at times been in a position that required courage, and you were surprised at the amount you showed. Now, when once you arouse yourself, you have this courage all the time and it is not necessary to have a special occasion reveal it. My object in so strongly impressing this on your mind is to make you aware that the same courage, the same determination that you show at certain exceptionable times, you have at your command at all times. It is a part of your vast resources. Use it often and well, in working out the highest destiny of which you are capable.

Father Time keeps going on and on. Every day he rolls around means one less day for you on this planet. Most of us only try to master the external conditions of this world. We think our success and happiness depend on us doing so. These are, of course, important, and I don't want you to think they are not; but I want you to realize that when death comes, only those inherent and acquired qualities and conditions within the mentality—your character, conduct, and soul growth—will go with you. If these are what they should be, you need not be afraid of not being successful and happy, for with these qualities you can mold external materials and conditions.

Now start from this minute to act according to the advice of the higher self in everything you do. If you do, its ever-harmonious forces will necessarily ensure a successful fulfillment of all your life purposes. Whenever you feel tempted to disobey your higher promptings, hold the thought: "My-higher-self-ensures-to-me-the-happiness-of-doing-that-which-best-answers-my-true-relations-to-all-others."

You possess latent talents, which when developed and used are of assistance to you and others. But if you do not properly use them, you shirk your duty, and you will be the loser and suffer from the consequences. Others will also be worse off if you do not fulfill your obligations.

Hold the thought: "I-will-live-for-my-best. I-seek-wisdom, self-knowledge, happiness-and-power-to-help-others. I-act-from-the-higher-self, therefore-only-the-best-can-come-to-me."

The more we become conscious of the presence of the higher self, the more we should try to become a true representative of the human soul in all its wholeness and holiness, instead of wasting our time dwelling on some trifling external quality or defect. We should try to secure a true conception of what we really are so as not to over value the external furnishings. You will then not surrender your dignity or self-respect when others ignorantly make a display of material things to show off. Only the person who realizes that he is a permanent Being knows what the true self is

ABOUT THE AUTHORS

"Theron Q. Dumont" was one of several pseudonyms used by WILLIAM WALKER ATKINSON, a popular and innovative New Thought writer and publisher in the early twentieth century. Born in Baltimore, Maryland, in 1862, Atkinson became a successful attorney in 1894. Following a series of illnesses, he immersed himself in New Thought literature. He soon became an important figure in the early days of the movement, publishing magazines such as *Suggestion, New Thought*, and *Advanced Thought*. Under the aegis of his own publishing company, Yogi Publication Society, Atkinson wrote many self-bylined works, and many titles under the pseudonyms Yogi Ramacharaka, Magus Incognito, Theron Q. Dumont, and Three Initiates. Under the last of these, Atkinson wrote his most popular and enduring work, *The Kybalion*. Published in 1908 by Atkinson's Chicago-based press, *The Kybalion* is perhaps the most widely read occult book of the twentieth century. Atkinson died in California in 1932.

MITCH HOROWITZ, who abridged and introduced this volume, is the PEN Award-winning author of books including *Occult America* and *The Miracle Club: How Thoughts Become Reality.* *The Washington Post* says Mitch "treats esoteric ideas and movements with an even-handed intellectual studiousness that is too often lost in today's raised-voice discussions." Follow him @MitchHorowitz.

Printed in the USA
CPSIA information can be obtained
at www.ICGtesting.com
JSHW012042140824
68134JS00033B/3218

9 781722 500597